❖ Favorite Family Menus ❖

Family Favorites

Vegie Burgers

Calories: 160
Fat: 3 grams
Cholesterol: 0 mg
Sodium: 304 mg
Makes 10 burgers

2 16-ounce cans garbanzo beans, rinsed and drained
vegetable oil spray
1 medium onion, finely chopped
1 large carrot, shredded
1 medium zucchini, shredded
1⅓ cups soft whole wheat bread crumbs
1 teaspoon paprika
1 teaspoon dried oregano, crushed
¼ to ½ teaspoon salt
freshly ground black pepper
2 egg whites, lightly beaten

1 Place beans in large mixing bowl. Coarsely mash with a potato masher. Set aside.
2 Spray a large skillet with vegetable oil spray. Add onion and carrot. Cook over medium heat until onion is tender. Transfer to bowl with mashed beans.
3 Add zucchini, bread crumbs, paprika, oregano, salt and pepper to bean mixture. Stir to combine. Stir in egg whites.
4 Using hands, form mixture into 10 patties. Place on a tray and cover with plastic wrap. Refrigerate at least 30 minutes before cooking.
5 Spray a baking sheet with vegetable oil spray. Place patties on baking sheet and broil patties 4 inches from the heat about 5 minutes per side or until golden brown.

Tangy Coleslaw

Calories: 24
Fat: 0 grams
Cholesterol: 0 mg
Sodium: 28 mg
Serves 10

12 ounces green cabbage, finely shredded
8 ounces red cabbage, finely shredded
1 large carrot, shredded
2 green onions, finely chopped
⅓ cup apple juice
2 tablespoons cider vinegar
1 teaspoon Dijon mustard

1 Place cabbage, carrot and onion in a large serving bowl. Use hands to combine thoroughly.
2 Place remaining ingredients in a small jar. Shake vigorously for 30 seconds or until combined. Pour over vegetables and toss lightly to combine. Serve immediately.

Note: Vegetables may be prepared and refrigerated until required. Dress coleslaw just before serving to keep vegetables crisp.

Spicy Chicken Kebabs

Calories: 135
Fat: 3 grams
Cholesterol: 58 mg
Sodium: 71 mg
Makes 10 kebabs

2 pounds boneless, skinless chicken tenderloins
1 cup plain nonfat yogurt
2 tablespoons finely chopped cilantro
1 teaspoon ground cumin
1 teaspoon ground coriander
2 teaspoons finely grated gingerroot
1 tablespoon curry powder
bamboo skewers

1 Trim chicken of excess fat. Cut tenderloins in half crosswise; place in a shallow non-metal dish.
2 Combine remaining ingredients and spread over chicken. Store, covered, in refrigerator for 2 hours, turning occasionally.
3 Drain meat and thread onto bamboo

FAVORITE FAMILY MENUS

Tangy Coleslaw (top) and Spicy Chicken Kebabs.

skewers. Grill the kebabs directly over medium-hot coals for 6 minutes per side or until no longer pink. Or, broil the kebabs 3–4 inches from the heat for 5 minutes per side.
Serve immediately.

Note: Boneless, skinless chicken breasts may be substituted for the tenderloins in this recipe, if desired. Trim the breasts of all fat and cut them into strips about ¾ inch wide and 2 inches long.

HINT
To avoid burning bamboo skewers on the grill or under the broiler, soak them in water for at least one hour before threading meat onto them.

❖ FAMILY FAVORITES ❖

Tomato Salad.

Tomato Salad

Calories: 26
Fat: 0 grams
Cholesterol: 0 mg
Sodium: 10 mg
Serves 10

5 *large ripe tomatoes*
2 *medium red onions*
1 *large cucumber*
¼ *cup balsamic vinegar*
⅓ *cup basil leaves*

1 Cut tomatoes into 1-inch cubes. Peel onions and slice thinly. Cut cucumber into ¾-inch cubes. Place in bowl.
2 Sprinkle balsamic vinegar over salad. Toss lightly to combine and refrigerate for at least one hour. Remove from refrigerator and allow to come to room temperature. Shred basil finely; toss with salad and serve immediately.

Note: Balsamic vinegar is an aged vinegar with a unique flavor. Look for it at grocery stores or specialty food shops.

Hint
For tomatoes with a full flavor, look for those marked 'vine-ripened'.

❖ FAVORITE FAMILY MENUS ❖

Corn Muffins.

Corn Muffins

*Calories: 109
Fat: 3 grams
Cholesterol: 1 mg
Sodium: 166 mg
Makes 12 muffins*

½ cup cornmeal
½ cup whole wheat flour
¾ cup all-purpose flour
2 tablespoons sugar
2 teaspoons baking powder
½ teaspoon baking soda
¼ teaspoon salt
6 oil-packed sundried tomatoes, patted dry and chopped
1 cup buttermilk
2 tablespoons sunflower or canola oil
2 egg whites, lightly beaten

1 Preheat oven to 350°F. In a large bowl stir together whole wheat flour, cornmeal, all-purpose flour, sugar, baking powder, baking soda and salt. Add tomatoes. Make a well in the center.
2 Stir together buttermilk, oil and egg whites. Add to flour mixture and stir until just combined.
3 Spoon batter into nonstick muffin cups. Bake for 20 minutes. Cool in pan for 5 minutes before carefully lifting out. Serve warm.

7

Family Favorites

Frozen Peach Ice

Calories: 68
Fat: 0 *grams*
Cholesterol: 0 *mg*
Sodium: 6 *mg*
Serves 10

3 16-ounce cans peach slices in natural juice
1 tablespoon honey
1 tablespoon vanilla
1½ teaspoons ground ginger

1 Place half of the undrained peaches and the honey, vanilla and ginger in food processor bowl. Using pulse action, press button for 30 seconds or until mixture is smooth. Pour into a large mixing bowl. Process remaining peaches and add to first mixture; stir to combine.
2 Divide mixture between two 8-inch deep, round cake pans. Cover with plastic wrap and freeze for 2 hours, until almost solid.

Working with one pan at a time, place mixture in large mixing bowl. Beat with electric beaters for 1 minute to break up large ice crystals. Return mixture to pan. Repeat with remaining mixture. Cover with plastic wrap and return to freezer for 2 hours.
3 Repeat beating process. Refreeze until just firm. Remove from freezer 5 minutes before serving.
4 To serve, place mixture in parfait glasses and accompany with a selection of fresh fruit.

Hint
Almost any fruit can be used instead of peaches. Fresh fruit and fruit juice can be substituted for canned fruit. Use a combination of fruit and juice to make up the weight which is required.

Frozen Peach Ice.

FAMILY FAVORITES

Celebration Dinner for 6

MUSHROOM PÂTÉ
SWEET POTATO SOUP
RATATOUILLE
HERB ROAST PORK
POTATO AND ONION CRISPS
STRAWBERRY MOUSSE

Mushroom Pâté

Calories: 101
Fat: 2 grams
Cholesterol: 3 mg
Sodium: 104
Serves 6

vegetable oil spray
1 small onion, *finely chopped*
1 clove garlic, *crushed*
⅓ cup *white wine*
20 ounces button mushrooms, *thinly sliced*
1 teaspoon dried thyme
½ cup *nonfat or low-fat ricotta cheese*
freshly ground black pepper

1 Spray a large saucepan with vegetable oil spray. Add onion and garlic and cook over medium-low heat until soft; add white wine, mushrooms and thyme. Cook, stirring occasionally, for 15 minutes or until very soft.
2 Reduce heat; cook 10 minutes more or until liquid has evaporated. Cool.
3 Place mushroom mixture, ricotta and pepper into food processor bowl. Using pulse action, press button 1 minute or until almost smooth.
4 Line a 3-cup capacity deep bowl with plastic wrap and spoon mixture into bowl. Press in firmly with the back of a spoon. Cover with plastic wrap and refrigerate for 1 hour, or spoon mixture into six individual serving bowls and refrigerate until set.
5 To serve, invert pâté onto a plate and serve with crackers or melba toast.

Mushroom Pâté (left) and Sweet Potato Soup (page 12).

❖ FAVORITE FAMILY MENUS ❖

FAMILY FAVORITES

Sweet Potato Soup

Calories: 148
Fat: 1 gram
Cholesterol: 0 mg
Sodium: 22 mg
Serves 6

1 teaspoon sunflower oil
2 large leeks, thinly sliced
1 teaspoon finely grated gingerroot
1½ pounds sweet potatoes, cut into 1-inch cubes
1 teaspoon curry powder
4 cups water
yogurt and chopped chives, to serve

1 Heat oil in a large pan. Add leeks and cook over medium heat until soft. Add ginger and cook 2 minutes more.
2 Add sweet potatoes, curry powder and water. Bring to a boil; reduce heat. Cover and simmer for 20 minutes or till potatoes are tender, stirring occasionally. Remove from heat. Cool.
3 Using a blender or food processor, blend soup in batches until smooth. Return to pan and reheat to serve. Serve with a dollop of nonfat yogurt. Sprinkle with chopped chives.

Ratatouille

Calories: 89
Fat: 1 gram
Cholesterol: 0 mg
Sodium: 16 mg
Serves 6

vegetable oil spray
1 large onion, chopped
2 cloves garlic, crushed
3 slender eggplant
3 medium zucchini
1 medium red bell pepper
1 medium green bell pepper
2 large tomatoes
1 teaspoon dried basil

1 Spray a large skillet with oil. Add onion and garlic; cook over medium-low heat until soft, stirring occasionally. Cut eggplant and zucchini into ¾-inch thick slices; cut bell pepper into ¾-inch squares. Add zucchini and bell pepper to onion mixture and cook 5 minutes or until just soft.
2 Cut tomatoes into 1-inch pieces; add to skillet with basil. Cover and cook over low heat for 5 minutes, stirring occasionally.
3 Uncover pan; cook 5 minutes more, stirring occasionally, until some liquid has evaporated. Serve immediately.

Herb Roast Pork

Calories: 204
Fat: 7 grams
Cholesterol: 90 mg
Sodium: 67 mg
Serves 6

2 1-pound pork tenderloins
½ cup firmly packed parsley leaves
¼ cup basil leaves
¼ cup mint leaves
1 tablespoon chopped chives
2 cloves garlic, quartered
2 teaspoons olive oil
freshly ground black pepper, to taste

1 Preheat oven to hot 425°F. Trim meat of excess fat. Place herbs, garlic and oil in processor bowl. Using pulse action, press button for 20 seconds or until mixture is almost smooth.
2 Butterfly each tenderloin and lay out flat. Cover with plastic wrap and pound to ¼- to ½-inch thickness. Spread each loin with herb mixture; roll up from long side. Tie with string.
3 Place meat on rack in a large baking dish. Sprinkle with black pepper. Bake 35–45 minutes or until slightly pink in center and thermometer registers 160°F. Remove from oven and let stand 5 minutes. Remove string before slicing.

From top: Ratatouille, Herb Roast Pork and Potato and Onion Crisps.

Potato and Onion Crisps

Calories: 183
Fat: 2 grams
Cholesterol: 0 mg
Sodium: 38 mg
Serves 6

6 small russet potatoes
1 small onion
2 teaspoons olive oil
1 teaspoon Dijon mustard
2 teaspoons finely shredded orange peel

1 Preheat oven to moderate 350°F. Peel the potatoes and slice them very thinly. Peel and slice onion very thinly. Combine potatoes and onions in a large mixing bowl.
2 Combine oil, mustard and peel. Add to the potato mixture. Using hands, toss thoroughly to combine.
3 Spread potatoes on a nonstick baking sheet or pizza pan. Bake for 30–45 minutes or until golden. Serve immediately.

FAMILY FAVORITES

For Strawberry Mousse: Add gelatin mixture to blended strawberry mixture.

Beat egg whites in a small bowl until soft peaks form.

✧ FAVORITE FAMILY MENUS ✧

Strawberry Mousse

Calories: 110
Fat: 1 gram
Cholesterol: 1 mg
Sodium: 58 mg
Serves 6

vegetable oil spray
8 ounces strawberries
2 cups nonfat or low-fat strawberry yogurt
2 teaspoons honey
1 envelope unflavored gelatin
2 tablespoons water
8 ounces strawberries, extra

Meringues
1 egg white
¼ cup sugar

1 Lightly spray a 3- or 4-cup ring or decorative mold with vegetable oil.
2 Place strawberries, yogurt and honey in food processor bowl. Using pulse action, press button for 30 seconds or until smooth.
3 Combine gelatin and water in a small bowl. Stand bowl in boiling water; stir until dissolved. Add to yogurt mixture. Process 5 seconds more or until combined. Pour into prepared ring mold and refrigerate 2 hours, or until set.
4 To make Meringues: Preheat oven to slow 300°F. Spray a baking sheet with vegetable oil spray. Place egg white in a small dry mixing bowl. Using electric beaters, beat egg white until soft peaks form. Add sugar gradually, beating until mixture is thick and glossy and all the sugar is dissolved.
5 Spoon mixture into a piping bag fitted with a large fluted nozzle; pipe 18 small round meringues onto prepared baking sheet. Bake for 30 minutes, until pale and crisp. Turn oven off. Cool meringues completely on baking sheet in oven, with the door slightly ajar.
6 To serve, invert mousse carefully onto serving platter. Surround with some of the meringues, and extra strawberries. Serve the remaining meringues separately.

HINT
Instead of using strawberries, try other berries, such as raspberries, blueberries or blackberries, if they are available. Frozen berries can be purchased from the freezer section of most supermarkets.

Strawberry Mousse.

Spoon meringue mixture into piping bag; pipe rounds onto baking sheet.

To serve, invert mousse onto serving platter; surround with meringues.

❖ FAMILY FAVORITES ❖

Spicy Buffet for 8

RED LENTIL DIP
BEEF CURRY
CARROT AND POPPYSEED SALAD
CUCUMBER AND MELON SALAD
CINNAMON POACHED PEARS
WITH VANILLA YOGURT

Red Lentil Dip

Calories: 133
Fat: 1 gram
Cholesterol: 0 mg
Sodium: 4 mg
Serves 8

1½ cups red lentils
1 teaspoon olive oil
1 clove garlic, crushed
1 medium onion, finely chopped
½ teaspoon ground ginger
1 teaspoon turmeric
1 teaspoon garam masala
2 cups water

1 Place lentils in a colander and rinse under running water. Drain well. Heat oil in a medium saucepan; add garlic and onion and cook over low heat until soft. Add ginger, turmeric and garam masala and cook and stir 1 minute more.
2 Add lentils and 2 cups water. Bring to a boil; reduce heat. Cover and simmer for 15–20 minutes, stirring occasionally. Be careful the mixture does not stick and burn. Transfer to a serving bowl to cool. Serve with toasted pita bread.

Note: You can buy garam masala at Asian markets or mix your own by combining ground cumin, ground coriander, black pepper, ground cardamom, ground cinnamon and ground cloves.

Beef Curry

Calories: 334
Fat: 11 grams
Cholesterol: 88 mg
Sodium: 324 mg
Serves 8

2½ pounds lean round steak
1 tablespoon peanut oil
2 large onions, chopped
1 tablespoon grated gingerroot
3 cloves garlic, crushed
1 tablespoon ground coriander
2 teaspoons ground cumin
½ teaspoon black pepper
1 teaspoon chili powder

Red Lentil Dip (top) and Beef Curry.

FAVORITE FAMILY MENUS

3 14½-ounce cans tomato puree
1 pound winter squash, peeled and cut into ¾-inch cubes

1 Trim meat of excess fat; cut into 1-inch cubes. Heat oil over medium-low heat in a large heavy saucepan. Add onions, ginger and garlic, cook gently for 10 minutes or until onions are soft, stirring occasionally.
2 Add coriander, cumin, pepper and chili powder; cook and stir for 2 minutes. Add tomato puree.
3 Add meat. Bring to a boil; reduce heat. Simmer, uncovered, for 45 minutes, stirring occasionally. Add the squash and cook 15 minutes more or until tender. Serve with rice and lavosh.

Fragrant Vegetables

Calories: 141
Fat: 3 grams
Cholesterol: 0 mg
Sodium: 159 mg
Serves 8

1 tablespoon olive oil
1 large onion, finely chopped
2 cloves garlic, crushed
1 teaspoon chopped fresh chili
1 cinnamon stick
2 teaspoons ground coriander
2 teaspoons ground cumin
1 medium eggplant, cut into ¾-inch cubes
3 medium carrots, sliced
6 ounces sweet potato, cut into ½-inch cubes
1 16-ounce can garbanzo beans, rinsed and drained
1 cup frozen green beans
2 zucchini, cut into ¾-inch cubes
½ cup boiling water
1 large tomato, chopped
1 tablespoon chopped parsley
1 tablespoon chopped cilantro

1 Heat oil in a large saucepan; add onion, garlic and cinnamon stick and cook for 2 minutes or until onion is soft. Add chili, coriander, cumin, eggplant, carrots and sweet potato. Cover; cook over a low heat for 10 minutes, stirring occasionally.
2 Add garbanzo beans, frozen beans, zucchini and water; stir to combine. Bring to a boil; reduce heat. Cover and simmer for 15 minutes. Add tomato and cook, uncovered, 5 minutes more. Stir in herbs and serve with rice.

Cucumber and Melon Salad

Calories: 43
Fat: 0 grams
Cholesterol: 0 mg
Sodium: 9 mg
Serves 8

1 medium cantaloupe
2 large cucumbers
2 small red onions
1 tablespoon chopped parsley

1 Cut cantaloupe in half. Scoop out seeds, peel and cut flesh into 1-inch cubes. Repeat with cucumbers, leaving skin on. Place in a serving bowl.
2 Chop onions finely, and add to bowl with parsley. Toss well to combine. Cover and refrigerate for 1 hour before serving.

Cucumber and Melon Salad (top) and Fragrant Vegetables.

Favorite Family Menus

FAMILY FAVORITES

Carrot and Poppyseed Salad

Calories: 68
Fat: 1 gram
Cholesterol: 0 mg
Sodium: 13 mg
Serves 8

3 large carrots
½ cup golden raisins
2 tablespoons poppyseeds
2 tablespoons lemon juice
2 tablespoons orange juice
1 tablespoon honey

1 Finely shred carrots and place in a serving bowl. Add golden raisins and poppyseeds; toss to combine.
2 Combine juices and honey, pour over carrot mixture. Stir until well coated. Cover and refrigerate until required.

Cinnamon Pears with Vanilla Cream

Calories: 165
Fat: 1 gram
Cholesterol: 1 mg
Sodium: 21 mg
Serves 8

3 cups natural pear or apple juice
2 cups water
8 medium pears
3 cinnamon sticks
2 tablespoons sherry

Vanilla Cream
1 cup nonfat or low-fat vanilla yogurt
2 teaspoons honey

1 Place juice and water in a large saucepan. Bring to a boil. Peel pears, leaving stalks intact. Place in boiling juice mixture. Return to a boil; reduce heat. Cover and simmer for 20 minutes, turning occasionally. Do not overcook. Pears should retain their shape. Remove from pan; cool at room temperature.
2 To make Vanilla Cream: Combine ingredients. To serve, place a pear on each plate with a dollop of Vanilla Cream.

Carrot and Poppyseed Salad (left) and Cinnamon Pears with Vanilla Cream.

FAMILY FAVORITES

Main Meals

Healthy food can be hearty and delicious, as well as nourishing. In this chapter are all the old favorites—roast lamb, baked fish, pizza and lasagna, to name but a few. However, the cooking methods and ingredients have been modified to follow today's guidelines for healthy eating.

Sweet and Sour Chicken

Calories: 251
Fat: 5 grams
Cholesterol: 72 mg
Sodium: 314 mg
Serves 6

1½ pounds boneless, skinless chicken breasts
2 green onions, chopped
1 strip lemon peel
6 black peppercorns

Sauce
1 teaspoon vegetable oil
1 tablespoon grated gingerroot
2 small onions, quartered
2 large carrots, thinly sliced
2 stalks celery, sliced diagonally
1 small red bell pepper, sliced

15¼-ounce can pineapple tidbits in natural juice (drain, reserve 1 cup juice)
¼ cup cider vinegar
2 tablespoons salt-reduced soy sauce
2 tablespoons tomato paste
1 tablespoon brown sugar
1 tablespoon lemon juice
4 teaspoons cornstarch
¼ cup chicken stock
1 small cucumber, halved lengthwise and sliced

1 Place chicken in medium saucepan and cover with cold water. Add lemon peel, green onions and peppercorns. Bring slowly to a boil. Reduce heat; simmer, covered, for 15 minutes or till tender and no longer pink. Remove chicken from saucepan. Reserve cooking liquid. Chill. Remove fat from

Sweet and Sour Chicken (top) and Vegetable Frittatas.

❖ MAIN MEALS ❖

surface of liquid. Slice chicken; cover, keep warm.
2 To prepare sauce: Heat oil in a large skillet. Add gingerroot and onion and cook over high heat 1 minute. Add carrot, celery and bell pepper; cook, stirring, 2 minutes.
3 Add pineapple juice, vinegar, soy sauce, tomato paste, sugar and lemon juice; stir to combine. Blend chicken stock and cornstarch; add and stir until mixture boils and thickens.
4 Add pineapple pieces, cucumber and chicken. Stir gently to combine. Serve with boiled or steamed rice.

Note: You can use any pre-cooked chicken but remember to remove all skin and fat.

Vegetable Frittatas

Calories: 115
Fat: 6 grams
Cholesterol: 142 mg
Sodium: 77 mg
Serves 6

1 tablespoon polyunsaturated margarine
3 green onions, chopped
2 small zucchini, sliced
4 ounces mushrooms, sliced
1 medium red bell pepper, chopped
1 8-ounce can low-sodium corn kernels, drained
4 eggs, lightly beaten
½ cup plain nonfat yogurt
1 tablespoon finely chopped basil

1 Preheat oven to moderate 350°F. Brush a 9-inch round quiche dish with a little melted margarine. Heat remaining margarine in large skillet; add green onions and cook until tender. Add zucchini, mushrooms, bell pepper and corn and cook over medium heat for 5 minutes more or until tender. Remove from heat. Drain off any excess liquid.
2 Combine eggs and yogurt in large bowl; add vegetables and basil. Mix well.
3 Pour mixture into prepared quiche dish. Bake 40 minutes or until set. Cut into wedges. Serve hot, warm or cold with a green salad.

Beef Stir-fry

Calories: 265
Fat: 11 grams
Cholesterol: 70 mg
Sodium: 440 mg
Serves 4

1 pound lean boneless round steak
1 tablespoon peanut oil
1 clove garlic, crushed
1 tablespoon grated gingerroot
3 green onions, diagonally sliced
2 carrots, sliced
1 medium zucchini, sliced
4 ounces mushrooms, sliced
3 ounces snow peas
2 tablespoons cornstarch

HINT
To make chicken stock, put 8 ounces chicken bones in a large saucepan. Add 1 small chopped onion, ½ small diced carrot, a few celery leaves, 2 peppercorns, a small bay leaf and 3½ cups water.
Simmer, uncovered, for 30 minutes, adding a little more water if necessary. Strain stock. Allow to cool completely, then remove any traces of fat from the surface.
Use as required. Leftover stock can be frozen, if desired. Transfer to airtight container, seal, label and date. Freeze, using within eight weeks.

Main Meals

Beef Stir-fry.

3 tablespoons water
2 tablespoons salt-reduced soy sauce
2 tablespoons sweet chili sauce

1 Trim meat of excess fat. Cut into thin strips.
2 Heat oil in large skillet or wok over medium heat. Add oil, garlic and green onions. Cook over medium heat 3 minutes or until golden.
3 Increase heat to high. Add beef; stir-fry for 3 minutes or until browned. Add carrots, zucchini, mushrooms and snow peas and stir-fry for 3 minutes.
4 Combine cornstarch, water, soy sauce and chili sauce in small bowl. Add to pan and stir until smooth. Cook, stirring, until sauce boils and thickens. Serve with brown or white rice.

Family Favorites

✦ MAIN MEALS ✦

Quiche Lorraine

Calories: 141
Fat: 5 grams
Cholesterol: 119 mg
Sodium: 248 mg
Serves 6

vegetable oil spray
4 sheets phyllo dough
3 eggs, lightly beaten
½ cup plain nonfat yogurt
2 ounces lean ham, chopped
2 green onions, chopped
2 tablespoons finely chopped parsley
½ cup shredded reduced-fat Swiss cheese

1 Preheat oven to moderate 350°F. Spray a 9-inch round quiche dish with vegetable oil. Cut pastry sheets in half. Line quiche dish with pastry sheets. Cover with damp towel to prevent pastry from drying out.
2 Combine eggs, yogurt, ham, green onions, parsley and cheese in large bowl. Mix well.
3 Pour egg mixture gently over phyllo dough. Bake for 40 minutes or until set. Serve hot or cold, cut into wedges, with fresh salad greens.

Beef and Bean Burritos

Calories: 452
Fat: 17 grams
Cholesterol: 57 mg
Sodium: 623 mg
Serves 6

1 pound lean ground beef
1 medium onion, chopped
1 tablespoon ground cumin
1 tablespoon paprika
1 tablespoon ground coriander
¼ cup mild taco sauce
1 16-ounce can red kidney beans, rinsed and drained
12 lettuce leaves, shredded
3 tomatoes, sliced thinly
3 carrots, shredded
1 avocado, sliced thinly
½ cup plain nonfat yogurt
½ cup shredded nonfat cheddar cheese
6 low-fat flour tortillas

1 Add beef and onion to a large nonstick skillet. Cook over medium heat till the meat is brown, using a fork to break up any lumps as it cooks. Drain off fat. Add cumin, paprika and coriander; cook and stir for 2 minutes.
2 Add taco sauce and kidney beans and cook over medium heat for 5 minutes or until mixture thickens, stirring occasionally.
3 To serve, place 2–3 tablespoons of the meat mixture onto each tortilla. Top with lettuce, tomato, carrot, avocado, yogurt, and sprinkle with cheese. Roll up tortilla around filling and serve hot or cold. Garnish with cilantro, if desired.

Note: Instead of ground beef, try ground chicken or turkey. Your best low-fat choice is chicken or turkey using ground breast meat. Canned black beans can be substituted for the kidney beans. If you like hot and spicy burritos, add 1–2 chopped jalepeno peppers to the meat mixture.

Beef and Bean Burritos (top) and Quiche Lorraine.

FAMILY FAVORITES

For Roast Lamb: Cover top of lamb with mint, lemon and garlic mixture.

Cut the unpeeled potatoes and squash into even-sized pieces.

Roast Lamb with all the Trimmings

Calories: 324
Fat: 15 grams
Cholesterol: 79 mg
Sodium: 183 mg
Serves 12

1/3 cup chopped fresh mint
1 tablespoon olive oil
1 tablespoon lemon juice
2 teaspoons finely shredded lemon peel
1 clove garlic, crushed
1 5-pound leg of lamb, trimmed of fat
12 medium new potatoes, quartered
2 pounds butternut squash, peeled and cut into chunks
2 tablespoons cornstarch
1½ cups chicken stock

1 Preheat oven to moderately slow 325°F. Combine mint, oil, lemon juice, rind and garlic in bowl. Remove pinkish red layer from outer surface of meat. Place lamb on rack in a large baking dish. Insert a meat thermometer. Roast for about 2 hours for rare (140°), 2–3 hours for medium (160°), or 2½–3 hours for well-done (170°).
2 Place unpeeled pieces of potato and squash on rack in baking dish and start baking 1 hour before lamb will be ready. Cook until well browned.
3 Remove lamb from oven and set aside. Pour away any fat remaining in dish. Blend cornstarch and chicken stock, add to dish and stir about 3 minutes over low heat until gravy boils and thickens. Strain and keep warm.
4 Slice lamb; serve with potatoes, squash and gravy, accompanied by steamed green beans and carrot sticks flavored with freshly ground black pepper and lemon juice.

Hint
When buying lamb, look for meat with a pinkish red colour and a thin layer of white fat surrounding it. Lamb can be coated with the mint mixture and allowed to marinate overnight in the refrigerator. This will intensify the flavor and tenderize the lamb.

Roast Lamb with all the Trimmings.

When gravy has boiled and thickened, strain and keep warm.

Slice lamb and serve with gravy, potatoes, squash and other vegetables.

Fish and Chips

Calories: 623
Fat: 9 grams
Cholesterol: 48 mg
Sodium: 448 mg
Serves 4

- 6 potatoes, cut into thick wedges
- 2 tablespoons vegetable oil
- 4 (4 ounces each) perch fillets
- ⅔ cup all-purpose flour
- 1 teaspoon ground cumin
- 1 teaspoon paprika
- 2 egg whites, lightly beaten
- 2 cups cornflake crumbs

1 Preheat oven to moderately hot 375°F. Line two baking sheets with foil.
2 Brush potatoes with oil; place on prepared baking sheet. Bake 45 minutes or until crisp. Remove from oven and keep warm.
3 Meanwhile, pat fish fillets dry with paper towels. Combine flour, cumin and paprika. Toss fish lightly in seasoned flour; shake off excess. Dip fish into egg whites one at a time. Coat with crumbs, shake off excess. Place on prepared baking sheet. Bake for 15 minutes or until fish flakes. Serve fish and potatoes with fresh lemon wedges and parsley.

HINT
Use any white fish fillets in this recipe. Substitute fresh bread crumbs for cornflake crumbs.

Tuna Casserole

Calories: 380
Fat: 4 grams
Cholesterol: 31 mg
Sodium: 495
Serves 4

- 1 cup elbow macaroni
- 1 teaspoon vegetable oil
- 3 green onions, chopped
- 2 leeks, thinly sliced
- 2 6½-ounce cans water-pack tuna, drained
- 1 8¾-ounce can low-sodium corn kernels, drained
- 1 tablespoon finely chopped thyme
- 2 tablespoons cornstarch
- 1 13-ounce can evaporated skim milk
- ½ cup soft whole wheat bread crumbs
- 2 tablespoons grated Parmesan cheese

1 Preheat oven to moderate 350°F. Cook pasta in large pan of rapidly boiling water until just tender. Drain, set aside.
2 Heat oil in large skillet. Add onions and leeks; cook over medium heat for 2 minutes or until tender. Add tuna, corn and thyme and cook for 5 minutes.
3 Combine cornstarch and milk and stir until smooth. Add gradually to pan, stirring over medium heat 3 minutes or until mixture boils and thickens. Add pasta; cook until warmed through.
4 Spoon mixture into 6-cup capacity ovenproof dish. Combine bread crumbs and cheese. Sprinkle over pasta. Bake 20 minutes or until golden. Serve hot with fresh green salad and crusty bread.

Note: To make Macaroni Cheese, replace the tuna with one cup of grated reduced-fat cheese. Use any shape of pasta in this recipe. Macaroni Cheese contains 371 calories, 9 grams fat, 25 mg cholesterol, and 407 mg sodium.

Tuna Casserole (top) and Fish and Chips.

❖ MAIN MEALS ❖

Family Favorites

Crisp Crumbed Chicken with Tomato Salsa.

Crisp Crumbed Chicken with Tomato Salsa

Calories: 372
Fat: 7 grams
Cholesterol: 84 mg
Sodium: 356 mg
Serves 6

2½ to 3 pounds chicken pieces
1 cup all-purpose flour
1 teaspoon garlic powder
2 egg whites, lightly beaten
2 cups cornflake crumbs

Tomato Salsa
1 medium tomato, finely chopped
1 small red onion, finely chopped
1 tablespoon chopped fresh cilantro
1 tablespoon chopped fresh mint
2 tablespoons lemon juice
2 teaspoons finely shredded lemon peel
1 teaspoon brown sugar

1 Preheat oven to moderately hot 375°F. Line a baking sheet with foil. Trim the chicken of excess fat and remove the skin. Combine the flour and garlic powder on a sheet of waxed paper. Toss the chicken lightly in seasoned flour, and shake off the excess.
2 Dip chicken pieces into egg whites a few pieces at a time. Coat with crumbs, and shake off the excess. Arrange pieces on a prepared baking sheet. Bake 45–55 minutes or until no pink remains and the coating is crisp.
3 To make Salsa: Combine tomato, onion, cilantro, mint, juice, peel and sugar in medium bowl. Cover with plastic wrap. Chill in refrigerator. Serve with chicken and crusty bread.

✦ MAIN MEALS ✦

Beef Stroganoff.

Beef Stroganoff

*Calories: 204
Fat: 7 grams
Cholesterol: 48 mg
Sodium: 104 mg
Serves 6*

1 pound beef tenderloin or sirloin steak
⅓ cup cornstarch
1 tablespoon paprika
1 tablespoon vegetable oil
1 clove garlic, crushed
1 medium onion, sliced
4 ounces mushrooms, sliced
1 tablespoon Worcestershire sauce
1 16-ounce can peeled tomatoes with no added salt
1 tablespoon finely chopped parsley
8 ounces plain nonfat yogurt

1 Trim meat of excess fat and cut into thin strips. Combine cornstarch and paprika on sheet of waxed paper. Toss meat lightly in seasoned flour; shake off excess.
2 Heat oil in large nonstick skillet. Add garlic and onion; cook over medium heat for 2 minutes or until tender. Add meat in small batches; cook 5 minutes or until well browned. Return all meat to pan. Add mushrooms, Worcestershire sauce, tomatoes and parsley. Bring to boil; reduce heat. Simmer for 5 minutes.
3 Fold in yogurt just before serving. Serve immediately with noodles and salad.

HINT
Use 1 pound boneless, skinless chicken breast fillets in place of beef.

33

Family Favorites

Family-style Lasagna

Calories: 327
Fat: 12 grams
Cholesterol: 61 mg
Sodium: 494 mg
Serves 8

1 medium eggplant, thinly sliced
1 tablespoon salt
1 pound lean ground beef, turkey or chicken
1 large onion, chopped
1 red bell pepper, chopped
1 clove garlic, crushed
1 28-ounce can peeled tomatoes, no added salt
¼ cup tomato paste
1 carrot, sliced
4 ounces mushrooms, sliced
2 zucchini, sliced
¼ cup chopped fresh basil
6 whole wheat or regular lasagna noodles
vegetable oil spray
8 ounces nonfat or low-fat ricotta cheese
8 ounces mozzarella cheese made with skim milk, shredded
grated Parmesan cheese (optional)

1 Preheat oven to moderate 350°F. Sprinkle both sides of

Clockwise from top left: Spicy Bean Casserole with Cornmeal Topping (page 36), Family-style Lasagna, and Coq au Vin (page 37).

Family Favorites

For Spicy Bean Casserole: Slice green onions and fresh chili; cook until soft.

Add squash, zucchini, tomatoes, corn and kidney beans to pan.

eggplant slices with salt; let stand 30 minutes. Rinse and pat dry with paper towels.
2 In a large skillet cook ground meat, onion, bell pepper, and garlic over medium heat till meat is brown and onion is tender. Drain off excess fat. Stir in tomatoes, tomato paste, carrot, mushrooms, and zucchini. Bring to a boil; reduce heat. Simmer, uncovered, for 20 minutes. Stir in basil.
3 Meanwhile, cook lasagna according to package directions, except omit oil and salt. Drain. Spray a 13 x 9 x 2-inch baking dish with vegetable oil spray. Line bottom of pan with 3 lasagna noodles.
4 Spoon one-half of the meat mixture over noodles. Top with one-half of the eggplant, one-half ricotta cheese and one-half mozzarella. Repeat layers with remaining ingredients. Bake, uncovered, for 60 minutes or till bubbly. Let stand 10 minutes before serving. Sprinkle each serving with Parmesan cheese, if desired.

Spicy Bean Casserole with Cornmeal Topping

Calories: 231
Fat: 2 grams
Cholesterol: 27 mg
Sodium: 448 mg
Serves 8

1 teaspoon olive oil
4 green onions, sliced
2 cloves garlic, minced
1 small red or green chili pepper, finely chopped
1 16-ounce can kidney beans, rinsed and drained
1 14½-ounce can diced tomatoes
1 pound acorn or butternut squash, peeled and cut into 1-inch cubes
2 zucchini, cut into 1-inch pieces
1 9- or 10-ounce package frozen corn kernels

Cornmeal Topping
1 cup all-purpose flour
¾ cup cornmeal
2 teaspoons baking powder
¼ teaspoon salt
1 egg, lightly beaten
¾ cup skim milk
2 tablespoons finely chopped chives

1 Preheat oven to moderate 350°F.
2 Place oil in large saucepan. Add onions, garlic and chili pepper and cook over medium-low heat till onions are tender. Add kidney beans, undrained tomatoes, squash, zucchini and corn. Stir to combine.
3 Transfer mixture to a 3½-quart oven-proof dish. Cover and bake for 1 hour, stirring after 45 minutes.

❖ MAIN MEALS ❖

For topping, make well in center. Add milk and mix to soft dough.

Top bean casserole with 8 mounds of cornmeal mixture.

4 For topping, in a medium bowl stir together flour, cornmeal, baking powder and salt. Stir together egg and milk. Add to flour mixture with chives. Stir just until combined.
5 Remove dish from oven and drop spoonfuls of dough over hot vegetable mixture. Return to oven and bake, uncovered, for 20–30 minutes or till topping is done and golden brown. Let stand 10 minutes before serving.

Coq au Vin

*Calories: 377
Fat: 15 grams
Cholesterol: 125 mg
Sodium: 717 mg
Serves 4*

*1 tablespoon olive oil
2½ pounds chicken pieces, skin and fat removed
12 pearl onions, peeled
8 ounces small button mushrooms, stems trimmed
2 cloves garlic, crushed
2 ounces lean turkey ham, finely chopped
½ cup dry red wine
1½ cups fresh chicken stock
2 bay leaves
2 tablespoons cornstarch extra ¼ cup water
½ cup finely chopped parsley*

1 Heat oil in a heavy large skillet; add chicken pieces. Cook over high heat 2 minutes to brown, turning once. Reduce heat and cook 3 minutes more on each side. Remove from skillet; drain on paper towels.
2 Add onions and mushrooms to skillet; cook over medium heat until onions are brown. Remove and set aside.
3 Add garlic and turkey ham to skillet; cook for 2 minutes. Add wine, stock and bay leaves and bring slowly to a boil. Reduce heat, simmer.
4 Return chicken to skillet. Cover; simmer for 35 minutes or until chicken is no longer pink. Remove chicken from skillet and keep warm. Add blended cornstarch and ¼ cup water to pan. Stir constantly until sauce boils and thickens. Return chicken, add onions and mushrooms and reheat. Discard bay leaves.
5 Place Coq au Vin onto serving plate and top with parsley. Serve with steamed new potatoes and snow peas.

Note: Turkey ham is made from turkey thigh, smoked and cured to look and taste like ham. It is available from delicatessens and supermarkets. If unavailable, use lean ham instead.

Burgers with the Works

Calories: 365
Fat: 12 grams
Cholesterol: 56 mg
Sodium: 477 mg
Serves 6

1 pound lean ground beef
½ cup soft whole wheat bread crumbs
3 green onions, chopped
1 tablespoon teriyaki sauce
6 whole grain hamburger buns
6 lettuce leaves
2 tomatoes, sliced
6 canned beet slices, drained
6 canned pineapple slices, drained

Relish
1 small onion, chopped
2 ripe tomatoes, chopped
1 tablespoon brown sugar
1 tablespoon tarragon vinegar

1 Combine ground beef, bread crumbs, green onions and teriyaki sauce in large bowl. Mix well. Shape meat mixture into six patties. Arrange patties on foil-lined baking sheet. Broil 3–4 inches from the heat for 5 minutes; turn and broil 5 minutes more or until browned and tender. Transfer to plate; keep warm.
2 Place buns, cut side up, under hot broiler 2–3 minutes or until lightly toasted. Top one half of each roll with beef patty. Place lettuce, tomato, beet slice and pineapple on top. Place remaining bun on top. Serve with Relish.
3 To make Relish: Combine all ingredients in medium pan. Cook over medium heat for 15 minutes or until liquid is absorbed. Cool before serving.

Beef and Vegetable Kebabs

Calories: 192
Fat: 6 grams
Cholesterol: 63 mg
Sodium: 499 mg
Serves 6

1¼ pounds boneless beef sirloin steak
⅓ cup salt-reduced soy sauce
2 tablespoons red wine vinegar
1 clove garlic, crushed
1 tablespoon grated gingerroot
2 onions, cut into quarters
1 large red bell pepper, seeded and cut into large cubes
½ small fresh pineapple, peeled and cut into chunks

1 Trim meat of excess fat. Cut into 1-inch cubes. Combine soy sauce, vinegar, garlic and gingerroot in large bowl. Add meat and stir to combine. Store meat mixture, covered with plastic wrap, in refrigerator several hours or overnight. Drain meat and reserve the marinade.
2 Thread meat, onions, bell pepper and pineapple alternately onto skewers.
3 Place kebabs on unheated broiling rack. Broil 3 inches from the heat for 5–6 minutes, or until meat is tender, brushing occasionally with reserved marinade.
4 Serve kebabs warm with boiled long grain or brown rice. Garnish with parsley, if desired.

Note: Vegetables must be cut slightly thicker than the meat so they don't overcook. A lean cut of pork, such as pork tenderloin, could be used instead of the beef in this recipe.

Burgers with the Works (top) and Beef and Vegetable Kebabs.

❖ MAIN MEALS ❖

Spaghetti and Meatballs

Calories: 454
Fat: 6 grams
Cholesterol: 65 mg
Sodium: 167 mg
Serves 6

vegetable oil spray
1 clove garlic, crushed
1 onion, chopped
1 large carrot, chopped
2 pounds ripe tomatoes, skinned and chopped
1/4 cup tomato paste
1/3 cup dry white wine
1/3 cup chicken stock
1 pound ground veal or lean ground beef
2 tablespoons cornstarch
1 egg white
1/2 cup finely chopped basil leaves
1 pound spaghetti

1 To make sauce: Spray a medium saucepan with vegetable oil. Place garlic, onion and carrot in saucepan. Cook over low heat until onion is soft. Add tomatoes, paste, wine and stock; bring slowly to a boil. Reduce heat, cover and simmer for 15 minutes. Remove from heat and cool slightly. Puree mixture in blender or food processor. Return to pan.
2 To make meatballs: Place veal, cornstarch, egg white and basil in medium mixing bowl. Mix well. Roll mixture into walnut-sized balls. Place balls into simmering sauce; cover and cook for 15 minutes.
3 To cook pasta: Place spaghetti in large pan of boiling water and cook until just tender. Drain.
4 Place pasta on serving plate; top with meatballs and sauce and garnish with fresh basil leaves.

Note: Regular or whole wheat spaghetti or any shape pasta can be used for this recipe. If desired, a little freshly grated Parmesan cheese may be sprinkled on top just before serving.

Family Pizza

Calories: 393
Fat: 11 grams
Cholesterol: 48 mg
Sodium: 566 mg
Serves 4

Crust
1/2 cup whole wheat flour
1 1/4 to 1 3/4 cups all-purpose flour
1 teaspoon dried oregano, crushed
1 package active dry yeast
1/4 teaspoon salt
2/3 cup warm water (120–130°F)
1 teaspoon olive oil

Topping
12 ounces ground chicken or turkey
1 onion, finely chopped
1 small green bell pepper, finely chopped
4 ounces mushrooms, sliced
1 clove garlic, crushed
1 14 1/2-ounce can diced tomatoes
3 tablespoons tomato paste
2 teaspoons dried oregano, crushed
1/2 cup shredded mozzarella cheese
8 black pitted olives, sliced

1 Preheat oven to hot 425°F, and lightly grease a 12-inch pizza pan.
2 In a large bowl combine whole wheat flour, half of the all-purpose flour, oregano, yeast and salt. Add warm water and oil. Beat with an electric mixer for 30 seconds. Beat on high for 3 minutes. Using a spoon, stir in as much remaining flour as you can. Knead on a lightly floured surface until smooth and elastic (6–8 minutes total). Cover and let rest 10 minutes.
3 With oiled fingers, pat the dough into the bottom and up the side of the prepared pizza pan. For thin pizza, do

❖ MAIN MEALS ❖

Family Pizza (left) and Spaghetti and Meatballs.

not let the dough rise. For thick pizza, cover and let rise in a warm place until nearly double (30–45 minutes). Bake for 12 minutes for thin pizza and 15–20 minutes for thick pizza or until light brown.

4 To prepare Topping: In a large skillet cook ground meat, onion, bell pepper, mushrooms and garlic over medium heat until meat is brown and onion is tender. Drain off fat. Stir in tomatoes, tomato paste and oregano. Bring to a boil; reduce heat. Simmer, uncovered, until thickened.
5 Spread topping over crust. Top with cheese and olives. Bake 10–20 minutes more or till topping is bubbly. Cut into wedges to serve.

41

Family Favorites

MAIN MEALS

Pork and Fruit Casserole

Calories: 406
Fat: 13 grams
Cholesterol: 89 mg
Sodium: 90 mg
Serves 6

1/3 cup all-purpose flour
1 1/2 pounds pork tenderloin, trimmed of fat and diced
4 medium green apples, peeled and cut into eighths
4 ounces dried apricots
4 ounces pitted prunes
1 cup apple juice
2 teaspoons coarse grain mustard
2 tablespoons lemon juice

1 Preheat oven to moderate 350°F.
2 Place flour in a large plastic bag. Add pork; seal bag and shake until all meat is evenly coated with flour. Shake off excess.

HINT
Dried apples may be used in place of fresh. If using dried apples, add an extra 1/4 cup apple juice. If using fresh apples, choose firm and crisp Granny Smith apples for the best results.

3 Place meat and fruit in layers in ovenproof dish, ending with a layer of fruit.
4 Combine apple juice, mustard and lemon juice. Pour over meat and fruit. Cover, bake for 1 hour. Serve accompanied by pasta and crisp green salad.

Vegetable Risotto

Calories: 340
Fat: 4 grams
Cholesterol: 3 mg
Sodium: 151 mg
Serves 4

1 teaspoon olive oil
1 large onion, chopped
1 1/4 cups Arborio or short-grain rice
1/4 cup dry white wine
4 to 5 cups hot low-sodium chicken stock
1/2 cup frozen peas
1/2 cup frozen corn kernels
4 ounces button mushrooms, sliced
2 large tomatoes, peeled, seeded and chopped
1/2 teaspoon freshly ground black pepper
1 teaspoon finely shredded lemon peel
1 tablespoon lemon juice
2 tablespoons grated Parmesan cheese

1 Heat oil in medium saucepan. Add onion; stir over medium heat until golden; add rice.
2 Reduce heat to low; stir rice 3 minutes or until lightly golden. Add wine and 1 cup of the stock to the pan. Stir continuously for 6 minutes or until all the liquid is absorbed.
3 Repeat process, stirring continuously, until all liquid has been added and rice is almost tender. Add vegetables; stir to combine. Cover and cook for 5 minutes.
4 Remove from heat. Stand, covered, 3 minutes. Stir in pepper, peel, lemon juice and cheese. Serve immediately.

Note: Rice requires constant stirring to make it creamy and prevent sticking to the pan. It is best to use a heavy nonstick saucepan.

Pork and Fruit Casserole (top) and Vegetable Risotto.

Oven-roasted Potatoes

Calories: 158/153
Fat: 1 gram/0 grams
Cholesterol: 1 mg/0 mg
Sodium: 177 mg/35 mg
Serves 8

8 small white potatoes, washed (2 pounds)

Filling 1
1 6½-ounce can boneless, skinless salmon, drained and flaked
½ cup nonfat cottage cheese
1 tablespoon chopped chives
2 teaspoons lemon juice
1 teaspoon finely shredded lemon peel
¼ teaspoon freshly ground black pepper

Filling 2
1 cup frozen corn kernels
1 medium red bell pepper, seeded, chopped
1 stalk celery, chopped
½ cup plain nonfat yogurt
1 teaspoon coarse grain mustard

1 Preheat oven to moderate 350°F.
2 Place potatoes on baking sheet. Prick with a skewer and cook for 1–1½ hours, or until golden brown and tender.
3 For Filling 1: Place salmon, cottage cheese, chives, lemon juice, peel and pepper into medium mixing bowl. Stir to combine.
  For Filling 2: Place corn, bell pepper, celery, yogurt and mustard into mixing bowl. Stir to combine.
4 Remove potatoes from oven. Cut a lid from each potato. Carefully scoop out contents. Place in medium mixing bowl; mash until smooth and creamy. Set shells aside.
5 Divide mashed potato in half; add to each filling. Mix gently to combine. Pile mixture back into potato shells, replace lids and bake for 15 minutes more. Serve hot, accompanied by a tossed salad.

Note: The first set of figures given in the nutritional analysis is for Filling 1 and the second set is for Filling 2.

Paella

Calories: 280
Fat: 8 grams
Cholesterol: 51 mg
Sodium: 392 mg
Serves 6

1 teaspoon olive oil
1 medium red onion, chopped
1 small green bell pepper, chopped
1 small red bell pepper, chopped
1 pound boneless, skinless chicken thighs or breasts
2 cloves garlic, minced
1 cup long grain rice
2 cups chicken stock
2 medium tomatoes, chopped
1 teaspoon dried oregano, crushed
¼ teaspoon ground saffron or turmeric
1 9-ounce package frozen artichoke hearts or tiny peas, thawed
2 tablespoons chopped parsley

1 Trim chicken of excess fat. Cut into bite-size pieces. Place oil in a Dutch oven. Add onion and bell peppers and cook over medium heat till tender. Add chicken and garlic. Cook and stir till chicken is partially cooked. Stir in remaining ingredients except artichoke hearts and parsley.
2 Bring stock slowly to a boil; stir once. Reduce heat; cover and simmer for 20 minutes or until rice is tender.
3 Remove from heat. Stir in artichoke hearts and parsley. Let stand, covered, 10 minutes or until all liquid is absorbed. Serve warm with whole grain bread or rolls.

Oven-roasted Potatoes (top) and Paella.

❖ MAIN MEALS ❖

FAMILY FAVORITES

Desserts

For the sweet tooth, there are plenty of satisfying and healthy alternatives to fresh seasonal fruit. Nonfat and low-fat yogurt make a good substitute for fat-laden cream, and ricotta cheese is a low-fat filling in cheesecake and crepes. Skim milk and other low-fat products are also invaluable for the health-conscious.

Banana and Apple Cake

Calories: 369
Fat: 8 grams
Cholesterol: 0 mg
Sodium: 201 mg
Serves 8

vegetable oil spray
1/3 cup polyunsaturated margarine
1 cup sugar
2 egg whites
3 ripe bananas, mashed
2 apples, peeled, cored and chopped
2 1/2 cups all-purpose flour
1 tablespoon baking powder
1 teaspoon ground cinnamon
1/4 cup skim milk
sifted powdered sugar

1 Preheat oven to moderate 350°F. Spray an 8-inch bundt or tube pan with vegetable oil. In a medium bowl beat margarine and sugar with electric beaters until well mixed. Add egg whites, beating thoroughly. Fold in banana and apple. Set aside.
2 Combine flour, baking powder and cinnamon in a large mixing bowl. Make a well in the center.
3 Add banana mixture and skim milk alternately to dry ingredients. Stir until just combined.
4 Pour mixture into prepared pan. Smooth surface. Bake 50–60 minutes or until a toothpick inserted near the center comes out clean. Let cake stand 10 minutes in pan before turning onto wire rack to cool. Serve cake plain or with a light dusting of powdered sugar.

Banana and Apple Cake (right) and Lemon Meringue Pie (page 48).

❖ DESSERTS ❖

Lemon Meringue Pie

Calories: 251
Fat: 8 grams
Cholesterol: 27 mg
Sodium: 108 mg
Serves 8

Pastry
vegetable oil spray
1¼ cups all-purpose flour
⅛ teaspoon salt
¼ cup polyunsaturated margarine
1 tablespoon lemon juice
2–3 tablespoons water

Filling
½ cup sugar
⅓ cup cornstarch
1½ cups water
1 egg yolk
1 tablespoon polyunsaturated margarine
1 teaspoon finely shredded lemon peel
⅓ cup lemon juice

Meringue
¼ cup honey
2 egg whites

1 Preheat oven to moderate 350°F. Lightly spray a 9-inch round pie plate with vegetable oil. Place flour, salt and margarine in food processor bowl. Using pulse action, press for 10 seconds or until mixture is fine and crumbly. Add lemon juice and almost all the water. Process for 15 seconds or until mixture comes together. Add more water, if necessary. Form dough into a ball.

2 On a lightly floured surface flatten pastry and roll large enough to cover base and sides of pie plate. Cut a sheet of waxed paper large enough to cover pastry-lined pie plate. Spread a layer of dried beans or rice evenly over paper. Bake for 10 minutes. Remove from oven; discard paper and beans/rice. Return pastry to oven and bake 10 minutes more or until lightly golden. Remove from oven. Reduce heat to moderately slow 325°F.

3 To make Filling: Combine sugar and cornstarch in a medium saucepan. Stir in water. Stir constantly over medium heat until mixture boils and thickens; boil 2 minutes more. Remove from heat; cool slightly. Add egg yolk and beat well. Return to heat and bring to a gentle boil. Remove from heat. Stir in margarine and peel. Gradually stir in lemon juice.

4 To make Meringue: Place honey in small pan. Bring to boil; reduce heat and simmer 1 minute. Place egg whites in small dry mixing bowl. Using electric beaters, beat egg whites until soft peaks form. Add honey gradually, beating constantly until mixture is thick and glossy.

5 Pour hot filling into pastry shell. Spread or pipe meringue decoratively over the top. Bake 15 minutes or until meringue is golden. Cool on a wire rack. Cover and chill to store.

Note: To make orange meringue pie, replace lemon juice with orange juice and lemon peel with orange peel.

Caramel Soufflés

Calories: 205
Fat: 7 grams
Cholesterol: 54 mg
Sodium: 127 mg
Makes four ¾-cup soufflés

vegetable oil spray
2 tablespoons polyunsaturated margarine
¼ cup brown sugar
¼ cup all-purpose flour
2 tablespoons evaporated skim milk
1 egg, beaten
4 egg whites
¼ cup sugar

1 Preheat oven to moderately slow 325°F. Spray four ¾-cup soufflé dishes with vegetable oil. Heat margarine in medium pan; add sugar. Stir over low heat until margarine has melted and sugar dissolved.

❖ DESSERTS ❖

Caramel Soufflés.

2 Add flour, stir over low heat 2 minutes or until flour mixture is golden. Add milk gradually to pan, stirring until mixture boils and thickens. Boil 1 minute more; remove from heat. Add egg and beat until smooth. Transfer mixture to medium bowl.
3 Using electric beaters, beat egg whites in small dry mixing bowl until soft peaks form. Gradually add sugar, beating till stiff peaks form. Gently fold into caramel mixture.
4 Spoon into prepared dishes; place on baking sheet. Bake 15 minutes or until well risen and browned. Dust lightly with sifted powdered sugar. Serve immediately.

Family Favorites

❖ DESSERTS ❖

Miniature Fruit Flans

Calories: 283
Fat: 10 grams
Cholesterol: 72 mg
Sodium: 165 mg
Serves 6

vegetable oil spray
1¼ cups all-purpose flour
⅛ teaspoon salt
¼ cup polyunsaturated margarine
1 tablespoon lemon juice
2–3 tablespoons water

Filling
2 eggs, lightly beaten
1½ cups skim milk
¼ cup sugar
1 teaspoon vanilla

Topping
4 kiwi fruit, sliced
1 cup sliced strawberries

1 Preheat oven to moderate 350°F. Spray six 4-inch tart pans with vegetable oil. Place flour, salt and margarine in food processor bowl. Using pulse action, press button for 10 seconds until mixture is fine and crumbly. Add lemon juice and almost all the water. Process 20 seconds or until mixture comes together. Add more water, if necessary. Form dough into a ball. Wrap in plastic wrap and chill for 20 minutes.
2 Divide pastry into six equal portions. Roll pastry between two sheets of plastic wrap, large enough to cover base and sides of prepared pans.
3 Cut six sheets of waxed paper large enough to cover each pastry-lined pan. Spread a layer of dried beans or rice evenly over paper. Bake 10 minutes. Remove from oven, discard paper and beans/rice. Return pastry to oven and bake 5 minutes more or until lightly golden. Cool.
4 To make Filling: Combine eggs, milk and sugar in a medium saucepan. Stir over medium heat until mixture thickens and coats a metal spoon. Remove from heat. Add vanilla. Quickly cool by placing saucepan in sink or bowl of ice water for 2 minutes, stirring constantly.
5 Spoon custard mixture into pastry shells; top with fruit. Serve.

> **HINT**
> Use slices of banana or mandarin oranges to replace the strawberries and kiwi fruit if these are not in season.

Apricot Strudel

Calories: 191
Fat: 7 grams
Cholesterol: 1 mg
Sodium: 104 mg
Serves 6

4 sheets phyllo dough
2 tablespoons polyunsaturated margarine, melted
¼ cup ground almonds
2 16-ounce cans apricot halves in light syrup, drained
¼ cup nonfat ricotta cheese
¼ teaspoon ground cinnamon
1 tablespoon skim milk

1 Preheat oven to moderate 350°F. Line a baking sheet with parchment paper. Lay one sheet of pastry on top of another. Brush top with margarine, sprinkle with almonds.
2 Place remaining two sheets on top. Cover with damp towel to prevent drying out.
3 Combine apricots, ricotta and cinnamon in a food processor bowl. Pulse till well combined. Place filling along one edge of pastry, leaving ¾ inch at each side. Fold in sides and roll up. Place on prepared baking sheet. Brush with skim milk. Bake for 40 minutes or until golden. Serve warm.

Apricot Strudel (top) and Miniature Fruit Flans.

FAMILY FAVORITES

For Fruit Puffs: Add flour all at once to water and margarine mixture.

Stir until mixture thickens and comes away from side of the pan.

Desserts

Fruit Puffs

Calories: 120
Fat: 5 grams
Cholesterol: 55 mg
Sodium: 58 mg
Makes 12 large puffs

vegetable oil spray
1 cup water
¼ cup polyunsaturated margarine
1 cup all-purpose flour
3 eggs, lightly beaten

Filling
8 ounces nonfat ricotta cheese
1 teaspoon vanilla
⅓ cup powdered sugar
1 cup strawberries chopped
1 teaspoon powdered sugar, extra

1 Preheat oven to moderately hot 400°F. Spray a large baking sheet with vegetable oil.

2 Combine water and margarine in a medium saucepan. Stir over low heat until margarine has melted. Bring quickly to a boil. Add flour all at once. Using a wooden spoon, beat vigorously until mixture is smooth and comes away from the side and base of the saucepan.

3 Remove saucepan from heat and cool slightly. Add eggs, one at a time, beating with a wooden spoon after each addition until smooth.

4 Place spoonfuls of mixture on a baking sheet. Bake about 30 minutes or until puffs are well risen and golden brown.

5 Cool puffs in oven with door ajar for 15 minutes. Remove from oven. Cut each puff in half and, using teaspoon, remove any uncooked mixture.

Cool on wire rack.

6 To make Filling: Using electric beaters, beat ricotta cheese, vanilla and powdered sugar until the mixture is thick and creamy. Fold in chopped strawberries. Spoon filling into each puff; top with lid. Dust with powdered sugar and serve immediately. Garnish platter with fresh strawberries, if desired.

Note: To keep the bottoms of the puffs from getting soggy, fill the puffs just before serving. To store puffs, cool them on a wire rack and place them in a plastic bag so they won't dry out. Store the puffs in the refrigerator for up to 24 hours or freeze them for 1–2 months. To thaw frozen puffs, let them stand at room temperature for 10–15 minutes.

Fruit Puffs.

Drop spoonfuls of dough onto prepared baking sheet.

Fold the chopped strawberries into the ricotta cheese mixture.

Crepes with Tangy Orange Sauce

Calories: 261
Fat: 4 grams
Cholesterol: 108 mg
Sodium: 77 mg
Serves 4

Crepes
vegetable oil spray
2 eggs
1¼ cups skim milk
¾ cup all-purpose flour
1 tablespoon sugar
1 teaspoon finely shredded orange peel
1 teaspoon vegetable oil
½ teaspoon vanilla

Sauce
juice and rind of 4 oranges
2 tablespoons lemon marmalade
2 tablespoons Grand Marnier

1 Place all crepe ingredients in food processor bowl or blender.
2 Using pulse action, press button for 15 seconds or until ingredients are combined and mixture is free of lumps.
3 Spray a 6-inch skillet with vegetable oil. Place over medium heat. Pour 2–3 tablespoons batter into skillet; lift and tilt pan to spread batter. Cook 2 minutes or until underside is golden. Turn crepe over, cook other side. Transfer to plate; cover with a towel. Keep warm.
4 To make Orange Sauce: Place all ingredients in nonstick skillet and stir over medium heat. Bring to a boil; reduce heat and simmer 10 minutes. Fold crepes into quarters; add to pan in batches. Serve crepes warm.

Note: For a great filling idea: Mix 4 ounces nonfat ricotta cheese with ¼ teaspoon ground cinnamon and ¼ teaspoon ground cloves. Place 1 tablespoon mixture inside each crepe. Pour sauce over to serve.

Baked Cheesecake

Calories: 178
Fat: 5 grams
Cholesterol: 20 mg
Sodium: 42 mg
Serves 12

1¾ cups finely crushed shredded wheat biscuits
¼ cup brown sugar
2 tablespoons polyunsaturated margarine, melted
1 egg white, lightly beaten

Filling
2 10-ounce packages soft tofu
1 cup nonfat or low-fat ricotta cheese
1 cup sugar
2 tablespoons all-purpose flour
1 tablespoon lemon juice
1 teaspoon finely shredded lemon peel
1 egg, lightly beaten

1 Preheat oven to moderately slow 325°F. Line base of 9-inch round springform pan with waxed paper. In a food processor combine crumbs, margarine and egg white. Using pulse action, process till well combined. Press mixture firmly into base and halfway up sides of pan.
2 To make Filling: Place tofu, ricotta cheese, sugar, flour, juice and peel into food processor bowl. Using pulse action, press button for 15 seconds or until mixture is smooth. Add egg and pulse till just combined.
3 Pour mixture onto crust-lined pan. Bake for 1¼ hours or until a knife inserted near the center comes out clean. Remove from oven; cool 15 minutes. Loosen crust from sides of pan; cool 30 minutes more. Remove sides of pan. Cool completely. Chill before serving. Garnish with orange slices, if desired.

Baked Cheesecake (top) and Crepes with Tangy Orange Sauce.

❖ DESSERTS ❖

Family Favorites

Desserts

Orange and Passionfruit Mousse

Calories: 90
Fat: 0 grams
Cholesterol: 0 mg
Sodium: 7 mg
Serves 6

1 envelope unflavored gelatin
½ cup cold water
2 tablespoons all-purpose flour
¼ cup honey
1 cup orange juice
1 tablespoon lemon juice
½ cup hot water
½ cup passionfruit pulp

1 Sprinkle gelatin over cold water; set aside.
2 Combine flour and honey in small pan; add small amount of orange juice to blend to a smooth paste.
3 Add remaining orange juice, lemon juice and hot water. Stir constantly over medium heat until mixture boils and thickens. Remove from heat.
4 Add softened gelatin; stir until dissolved.
5 Pour mixture into a pan and refrigerate until just beginning to set.
6 Transfer mixture to large bowl and beat with electric mixers until mixture is light, airy and doubled in volume.
7 Fold in passionfruit pulp. Place mixture into one large or individual serving dishes. Refrigerate the mousse for 1–2 hours before serving.

Apple Pie

Calories: 285
Fat: 8 grams
Cholesterol: 0 mg
Sodium: 137 mg
Serves 8

Pastry
vegetable oil spray
2 cups all-purpose flour
¼ teaspoon salt
⅓ cup polyunsaturated margarine
2 tablespoons lemon juice
4–5 tablespoons water

Filling
6 cups peeled, cored and thinly sliced apples
½ cup sugar
1 tablespoon all-purpose flour
1 teaspoon finely shredded lemon peel
1 teaspoon ground cinnamon
1 egg white
½ teaspoon ground cinnamon, extra

1 Preheat oven to moderate 350°F. Spray a 9-inch pie plate with vegetable oil.
2 Place flour, salt and margarine in food processor bowl. Using pulse action, press button for 10 seconds until mixture is fine and crumbly. Add lemon juice and almost all the water. Process 20 seconds or until mixture comes together. Add more water, if necessary. Form dough into a ball.
3 Roll out two-thirds pastry on lightly floured surface until ¼ inch thick or large enough to cover base and sides of pie plate. Trim off excess.
4 To prepare Filling: Toss apples with sugar, flour, lemon peel and 1 teaspoon cinnamon. Spoon into pastry-lined pie plate.
5 Roll out remaining pastry and cut into strips. Place on top to form a lattice pattern.
6 Lightly beat egg white.
7 Brush lattice top with beaten egg white and sprinkle with ½ teaspoon cinnamon.
8 Bake for 1 hour or until apples are tender and pastry is golden brown.

Note: Serve pie warm with a scoop of nonfat vanilla frozen yogurt.

Apple Pie (left) and Orange and Passionfruit Mousse.

FAMILY FAVORITES

Pavlova Yogurt Roll

Calories: 115
Fat: 1 gram
Cholesterol: 1 mg
Sodium: 49 mg
Serves 6

vegetable oil spray
4 egg whites
1/2 cup sugar
1 teaspoon cornstarch
1 teaspoon white vinegar

Filling
1/4 cup plain nonfat yogurt
1/4 cup nonfat ricotta cheese
2 tablespoons powdered sugar
1/2 teaspoon vanilla
1/4 cup fresh passionfruit pulp
1 cup strawberries, sliced

1 Preheat oven to moderate 350°F. Spray a 15 x 10 x 1-inch jelly-roll pan with vegetable oil. Line base with waxed paper; spray paper with oil. Dust with sifted powdered sugar; shake off excess.
2 Place egg whites in small dry mixing bowl. Using electric beaters, beat egg whites until soft peaks form. Add sugar gradually, beating constantly until mixture is thick and glossy and all the sugar is dissolved.
3 Fold in cornstarch and vinegar. Spread mixture into prepared pan. Bake for 12–15 minutes or until well risen and golden brown.
4 Turn meringue onto a sheet of waxed paper that has been lightly dusted with powdered sugar. Leave to cool to lukewarm.
5 To make Filling: Using electric beaters, beat yogurt, ricotta cheese, powdered sugar and vanilla until creamy. Chill till ready to use. Spread filling evenly over meringue and top with fruit. Using paper as guide, roll up from short side. Cover and chill till serving time. Cut into slices to serve.

Note: Meringue roll can be made a day ahead. Cover loosely with plastic wrap in refrigerator. Chill filling well before using. Meringue needs to be lukewarm for rolling, or it will crack.

Pavlova Yogurt Roll.

For Pavlova Yogurt Roll: Beat egg whites, adding sugar gradually.

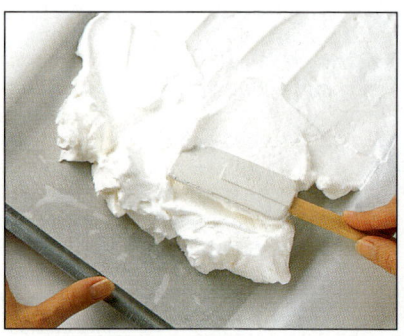

Spread meringue mixture onto prepared pan; bake until golden brown.

❖ **DESSERTS** ❖

Turn cooked meringue onto a sheet of waxed paper; leave to cool.

Spread filling over meringue and roll up carefully from short side.

59

Family Favorites

◆ DESSERTS ◆

Baked Rice Custard

*Calories: 197
Fat: 2 grams
Cholesterol: 73 mg
Sodium: 90 mg
Serves: 6*

⅓ cup long grain rice
2 eggs, lightly beaten
½ cup maple syrup
1 12-ounce can evaporated skim milk
¼ cup golden raisins
¼ teaspoon ground cinnamon

1 Preheat oven to moderately slow 325°F.
2 Cook rice in ⅔ cup boiling water in a medium pan about 15 minutes or until just tender.
3 Whisk together eggs, syrup and milk. Stir in rice and raisins.
4 Pour mixture into an 8-inch round or square ovenproof dish. Sprinkle with cinnamon.
5 Place dish into a deep baking dish. Pour in enough hot water to come halfway up the sides. Bake 50–55 minutes or until custard is set and a knife inserted near the center comes out clean. Remove from water immediately. Serve warm. Chill to store.

Marinated Strawberries with Yogurt Maple Cream

*Calories: 208
Fat: 6 grams
Cholesterol: 1 mg
Sodium: 37 mg
Serves 4*

⅓ cup currant or raspberry liqueur
1 tablespoon brandy
2 cups halved strawberries

Maple Cream
1 cup nonfat vanilla yogurt
1 tablespoon maple syrup
¼ cup pecans, chopped

1 Combine liqueur and brandy in a medium bowl.
2 Add strawberries to mixture and stir until combined. Cover and refrigerate for 2 hours.
3 To make Maple Cream: Combine yogurt, syrup and pecans. Mix well.
4 Serve strawberries with Maple Cream.

Baked Rice Custard (left) and Marinated Strawberries with Yogurt Maple Cream.

Super Choc-liqueur Cake

Calories: 242
Fat: 2 grams
Cholesterol: 56 mg
Sodium: 152 mg
Makes 8 servings

2 eggs
2 egg whites
⅔ cup sugar
¾ cup all-purpose flour
2 tablespoons unsweetened cocoa powder
1 teaspoon baking powder
¼ teaspoon salt
2 tablespoons hot water
¼ cup chocolate-flavored liqueur or syrup
4 ounces dried apricots, chopped
⅔ cup water
8 ounces nonfat or low-fat ricotta cheese
½ cup powdered sugar
1 teaspoon vanilla
1 teaspoon powdered sugar, extra
1 teaspoon unsweetened cocoa powder

1 Preheat oven to moderate 350°F. Spray two 8-inch cake pans with vegetable oil spray. Line base with baking paper.
2 Using electric beaters, beat eggs and whites in small mixing bowl for 8 minutes or until thick and pale. Add sugar gradually, beating constantly until mixture is pale yellow and glossy. Transfer to a large mixing bowl.
3 In a small bowl combine flour, cocoa powder, baking powder and salt. Using a metal spoon, fold in flour mixture with hot water and liqueur quickly and lightly. Spread mixture evenly into prepared pans. Bake 25 minutes or until cakes are lightly golden and shrink away from side of pans. Let stand in pans 5 minutes before turning onto wire rack to cool.
4 Combine apricots and water in small pan. Bring to a boil; reduce heat. Simmer, uncovered, about 15 minutes or until apricots are tender and water has evaporated. Remove from heat. Beat with a wooden spoon to form a paste. Allow to cool.
5 Using electric beaters, beat ricotta and powdered sugar until thick and creamy. To assemble cake: Place first layer on a board. Spread with apricot paste. Top with half ricotta cheese. Place remaining cake on top.
6 Transfer to serving plate and top with remaining ricotta cheese mixture. Dust with combined 1 teaspoon powdered sugar and 1 teaspoon cocoa.

Frozen Soft-serve Yogurt

Calories: 100
Fat: 1 gram
Cholesterol: 1 mg
Sodium: 34 mg
Serves 6

1 tablespoon unflavored gelatin
2 tablespoons water
1 8-ounce container nonfat plain yogurt
1 16-ounce can sliced peaches in natural juices, drained
¼ cup honey

1 Combine gelatin with water in a small bowl. Stand in boiling water; stir until dissolved.
2 Place drained peaches in a food processor bowl. Using pulse action, process till smooth. Add yogurt, honey, and gelatin. Using pulse action, process 20 seconds.
3 Transfer mixture into shallow metal pan. Cover and freeze for 2 hours. Return mixture to processor bowl. Using pulse action, process for 3 minutes. Return mixture to metal pan; freeze 2 hours more.
4 Return mixture to food processor bowl. Using pulse action, process for 3 minutes. Serve immediately.

Super Choc-liqueur Cake (top) and Frozen Soft-serve Yogurt.

❖ DESSERTS ❖

Index

Page numbers in italics refer to pictures

Apple Pie 56, 57
Apricot Strudel 50, 51

Banana and Apple Cake 46, 47
Bean Casserole, Spicy, with Cornmeal Topping 34, 36
Beef and Bean Burritos 26, 27
Beef and Vegetable Kebabs 38, 39
Beef Curry 16, 17
Beef Stir-fry 24, 25
Beef Stroganoff 33
Burger with the Works 38, 39

Caramel Soufflés 48, 49
Carrot and Poppyseed Salad 20, 21
Cheesecake, Baked, 54, 55
Chicken Kebabs, Spicy, 4, 5
Choc-liqueur Cake, Super, 62, 63
Cinnamon Pears with Vanilla Cream 20, 21
Coleslaw, Tangy, 4, 5
Coq au Vin 34, 37
Corn Muffins 7
Crepes with Tangy Orange Sauce 54, 55
Crisp Crumbed Chicken with Tomato Salsa 32

Cucumber and Melon Salad 18, 19

Eggplant Dip 2, 3

Family Pizza 40, 41
Family-style Lasagna 34, 35
Fish and Chips 30, 31
Frozen Peach Ice 8, 9
Frozen Soft-serve Yogurt 62, 63
Fruit Flans, Miniature, 50, 51
Fruit Puffs 52, 53

Herb Roast Pork 12, 13

Lemon Meringue Pie 47, 48

Mushroom Pâté 10, 11

Orange and Passionfruit Mousse 56, 57

Paella 44, 45
Pavlova Yogurt Roll 58, 59
Potato and Onion Crisps 13
Pork and Fruit Casserole 42, 43

Potatoes, Oven-roasted, 44, 45

Quiche Lorraine 26, 27

Ratatouille 12, 13
Red Lentil Dip 16, 17
Rice Custard, Baked, 60, 61
Roast Lamb with all the Trimmings 28, 29

Spaghetti and Meatballs 40, 41
Strawberries, Marinated, with Yogurt Maple Cream 60, 61
Strawberry Mousse 14, 15
Sweet and Sour Chicken 22, 23
Sweet Potato Soup 11, 12

Tomato Salad 6
Tuna Casserole 30, 31

Vegetable Frittatas 23, 24
Vegetables, Fragrant, 18, 19
Vegetable Risotto 42, 43
Vegie Burgers 3, 4